Miss B Goes To Space

Based on a True Story!

Lane Bagby and
Meredith Bagby

PRINCIPIO

Published by Principio Books, LLC

ISBN: 978-1-62908-016-1
Library of Congress Control Number: 2025903341
First edition: 2025
Edited by Danielle Dispaltro & Josiah Blount

Public Domain Image Credits
Some images in this book were provided by NASA and are in the public domain. NASA does not endorse this book or its contents.

Disclaimer
This book is based on historical events and is intended for educational and informational purposes. Every effort has been made to ensure accuracy, but the authors and publisher do not guarantee the completeness of the information.

Printed in the United States of America
Published by Principio Books, LLC
Los Angeles, CA
www.principiobooks.com

"There is no easy way from the earth to the stars."

- Seneca

No matter how small we may feel in this big universe, each one of us can make a world of difference.

Peru, 1957. Deep in the lush rainforest, a curious little squirrel monkey lived high in the treetops with her mom, dad, and friends.

Each day, she explored the canopy, searching for tasty nuts and sweet berries.

One day, while she was playing, she spotted strange, scary creatures — humans. They chased her through the forest.

She hid in a bush, shaking with fright. Suddenly, a giant hand reached in and grabbed her! Her tiny heart thumped with fear.

Hunters tossed her into a cage and loaded her onto a boat with other monkeys. As the boat sailed away, she watched her beloved rainforest fade into the morning mist. The sea stretched on and on. Her heart ached. She cried for home.

At last, the long journey ended at a busy dock in a place called Miami. The hunters left her and the other monkeys at a pet store.

PETS

She didn't know where she was or what would happen next.

Days later, men from the US Navy paid the pet store owner and loaded all the monkeys onto a truck. "Where am I going now?" she wondered.

She and her friends were taken to a lab. The Navy men whispered words like "big mission," "rocket," "capsule," and "space," which made her ears perk up.

The scientists measured her heart rate and breathing. They flashed bright lights and played loud, startling noises. Sometimes, they just stared at her for hours!

Then things got even stranger.
They put her in a container that shot
up and down in the air, soaring and
dipping like a giant wave.

They spun her side to side like
a pinball. She learned to run
through mazes, earning a cookie
when she escaped.

The scientists adored her for being smart, loving, and sweet. Donald, one of her trainers, named her "Miss Baker," but soon everyone called her Miss B. She loved hugging Donald and getting cookies from him.

In the lab, Miss B made a new friend —
a monkey named Miss Able. They played together and shared treats.
Like Miss B, Miss Able was a favorite among the scientists.

One day, Miss B overheard the reason for all the training. She could hardly believe it. They were planning to send a monkey into space, and she was the top choice — along with Miss Able!

The idea of flying among the stars made her heart race with excitement and a touch of fear.

BAKER

The scientists wondered:
Could they send living creatures to
space and safely bring them back to
Earth? If so, they hoped humans might
make the same trip one day.

In 1957, the year Miss B arrived at the
lab, a Russian dog named Laika became
the first creature to orbit Earth.
Sadly, Laika didn't survive. That year,
Russia also launched the first satellite,
Sputnik, amazing the world.

In 1958, America sent a brave monkey named Gordo to space. He soared 310 miles above Earth for over eight minutes. But when it was time to come back, the capsule's parachute failed to open, and Gordo was lost at sea. Would Miss B meet the same fate? The thought made her shiver. She wanted to be brave, but she was scared.

In spring 1959, Miss B and Miss Able prepared for their big journey. Donald dressed them in tiny helmets and leather jackets.

They climbed into a capsule no bigger than a shoebox, with sensors taped to them to monitor their temperature, heart rate, and breathing.

On the morning of May 28, Miss B and Miss Able arrived at Cape Canaveral, Florida. This is where America's space agency, called NASA, launched rockets into space. The scientists placed them safely inside the top of a towering rocket...It was taller than any tree Miss B had seen. She held her breath as the countdown began: "Ten... nine... eight..." The rocket shook as fire burst from its engines, sending birds scattering.

Miss B rattled in her seat, heart pounding. Suddenly, she felt a huge blast beneath her. Clouds of smoke billowed as the rocket shot up into the sky!

Miss B's eyes widened; she had never felt anything like it. They raced through space at 16,000 miles per minute! Finally, their capsule broke free from the powerful rocket, and they slowed down.

Everything began to float! Onions, mustard and corn seeds, tiny Neospora parasites, E. coli, fruit fly pupae, yeast, and sea urchin eggs all drifted around them.

Miss B and Miss Able had escaped gravity, the force that pulls everything down to earth. They floated for almost 10 minutes! Soon it was time to head home. As they fell back to Earth, gravity's pull pinned them to the back of the capsule — a force 38 times stronger than normal.

Miss B felt like an elephant was sitting on her chest. It was so intense that they both fainted!

The capsule started gaining speed. As it blazed
through the sky, it heated up to nearly 3,000 degrees—
hot enough to melt metal! But Miss B and Miss Able
were safe inside.

Near Puerto Rico, Donald waited on a ship.
He watched the capsule streak through the
sky, its nose tilting down like a shooting star.
With a splash, it landed in the ocean.

At first, Donald and his crew feared the capsule had sunk. Then they spotted it bobbing on the waves. Divers rushed to pull it aboard.

Donald quickly pried open the capsule. He gently pulled out Miss B and Miss Able. At first, Miss B didn't move, and Donald held his breath, fearful that she was injured. Then, she opened her eyes and let out a squawk. Donald hugged her and gave them each a cookie.

News of their safe return spread fast. Cheers erupted at Cape Canaveral. A doctor checked on Miss B and Miss Able and announced, "Able/Baker perfect." The mission was a success!

Miss B and Miss Able became stars, appearing on TV and the cover of Life Magazine. People around the world fell in love with America's space monkeys.

Not long after their adventure, Miss Able didn't feel well. She got sicker and sicker...The doctors tried to save her, but she passed away. Miss B's heart ached.

Their mission, however, was a triumph, paving the way for America to send humans to space. Two years later, astronaut Alan Shepard became the second person — and the first American — to journey to the stars.

In 1962, Miss B fell in love and married a fellow squirrel monkey named Big George. Even Donald attended their big celebration.

In 1971, Miss B retired and moved to a NASA center in Huntsville, Alabama. Visitors loved meeting her and hearing about space. Miss B was so popular she received over 100 letters a day!

Each year, her space adventure was celebrated with a big party filled with balloons, laughter, and her favorite treat: strawberry gelatin with bananas.

Miss B spent many happy years in Huntsville. In 1984, at 27 years old, she passed away peacefully, setting a record as the oldest living squirrel monkey! The curious little squirrel monkey had lived an adventurous life, not only reaching the stars but also touching the hearts of everyone she met.

The Real Miss Baker

Miss Baker and her scientist friend

Wearing her special necklace

Showing off her award

More Miss Baker!

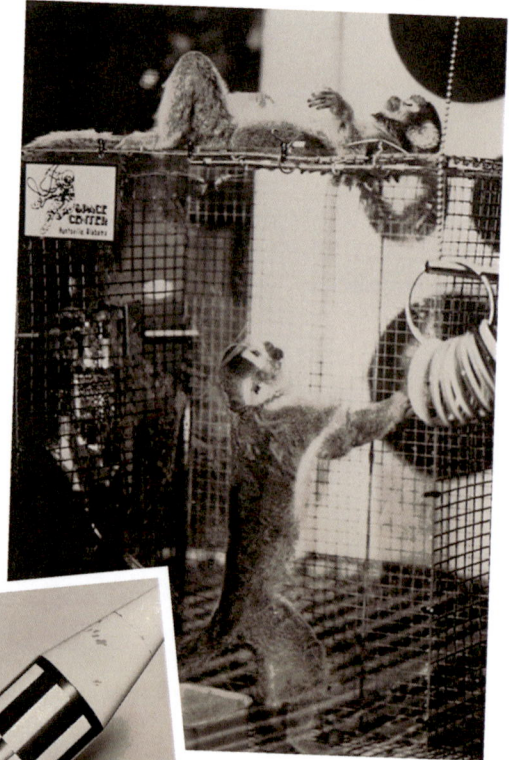

A party and cake for Miss Baker

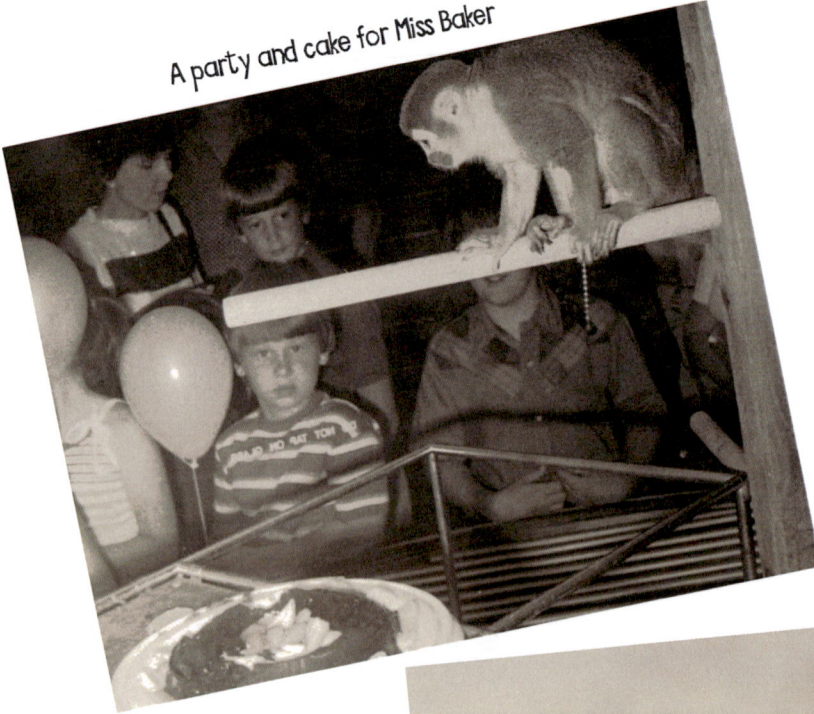

Miss Baker relaxing with her monkey friend

Riding a model rocket

www.ingramcontent.com/pod-product-compliance
Lightning Source LLC
Chambersburg PA
CBRC091801090426
42811CB00021B/1902